Fragments
in Us

The Felix Pollak Prize in Poetry

The University of Wisconsin Press Poetry Series
RONALD WALLACE, GENERAL EDITOR

Now We're Getting Somewhere ◆ David Clewell
Henry Taylor, Judge, 1994

The Legend of Light ◆ Bob Hicok
Carolyn Kizer, Judge, 1995

Fragments in Us: Recent and Earlier Poems ◆ Dennis Trudell
Philip Levine, Judge, 1996

Fragments in Us

Recent and Earlier Poems

DENNIS TRUDELL

The University of Wisconsin Press

The University of Wisconsin Press
114 North Murray Street
Madison, Wisconsin 53715

3 Henrietta Street
London WC2E 8LU, England

Library of Congress Cataloging-in-Publication Data
Trudell, Dennis.
    Fragments in us: recent and earlier poems / Dennis Trudell.
    84 p.   cm. — (Felix Pollak prize in poetry)
    ISBN 0-299-15210-3 (cloth: alk. paper).
    ISBN 0-299-15214-6 (pbk.: alk. paper).
    I. Title.
    PR6070.R7F73   1996
    821'.914—dc20   96-8243

for my father,
Charles Trudell ⎯⎯⎯⎯⎯⎯⎯⎯⎯⎯⎯⎯⎯⎯⎯⎯⎯⎯⎯

Contents

& Earlier

Acknowledgments _____

Aethlon: The Journal of Sports Literature ("Ballad of Jesse Howe," "Man with Baseball Mitt Outside Wrigley Field"); *America* ("The Artists"); *Context/South* ("Dushay's Friend"); *The Fiddlehead* ("The Jump Shooter"); *The Georgia Review* ("A Checkered Red and White Shirt," "Green Tomatoes," "The Light in Our Bodies," "Music," "Watch Them Die," "The Window"); *Green Mountains Review* ("God's Country"); *Isthmus* ("Gulf Legs"); *New England Review/ Bread Loaf Quarterly* ("A Small Black Album"); *North American Review* ("Father"); *Poetry* ("Epilogue"); *Prairie Schooner* ("Nicaraguan Village," as "The Rain That Falls . . . ," reprinted from the *Prairie Schooner* by permission of the University of Nebraska Press. Copyright 1984 by the University of Nebraska Press; "We All Came Out . . . ," reprinted from the *Prairie Schooner* by permission of the University of Nebraska Press. Copyright 1986 by the University of Nebraska Press); *TriQuarterly*, a publication of Northwestern University ("If It Dies," "Isthmus"); *Wormwood Review* ("The Guest").

Some poems in this book have appeared in the following anthologies and chapbooks: *Eleven Wisconsin Poets* (Kendall/Hunt); *The Glacier Stopped Here* (Isthmus Publishing Company); *The Guest* (Fiddlehead Books); *Imagining a Revolution* (Ojalá Press); *The Journey Home: Literature of Wisconsin* (North Country Press); *Keener Sounds: Selected Poems from the Georgia Review* (University of Georgia Press); *New Voices in American Poetry* (Winthrop); *A New White* (Chapbook Press); *Quickly Aging Here* (Doubleday/Anchor);

Straight from the Heart (Lonesome Traveller Publishing); *Wisconsin Poetry* (Wisconsin Academy of Arts, Sciences, and Letters).

"Fragment in Us" is based upon material from Howard Zinn's *A People's History of the United States* (Harper). "A Checkered Red and White Shirt," "If It Dies," and "Nicaraguan Village" were written to photographs in Susan Meiselas' *Nicaragua: June 1978–July 1979* (Pantheon). Respect and gratitude for this work.

Recent

Retain your indignant eye and stand with the accused.

NELSON ALGREN

Dushay's Friend

Dushay knifed between two punks, double-
pumped going up—and died; his friend
froze in the gunshots' echo as 'Shay
bounced off the post and left it smeared.
And left it smeared. The basketball rolled

west across State . . . and Dushay's friend
walked after it, and kept walking. Later
cops asked his name and nobody knew.
"Dushay's friend," " 'Shay's man, man," they
heard with shrugs. And shrugged. Never

found him or Little Truck's basketball
again. Dushay's friend walked due west
that day for six hours; and then he dribbled
two hours more and slept in a field.
Next morning the basketball glowed so

orange the smeared post in Dushay's
friend's mind was dulled—and he dribbled
the ball through a town. That night
it glowed the moon two towns away.
And a post there glowed. And Dushay's

friend's tears as he made 'Shay's shot.

"God's Country"

A family who slept in it spread clothes
and toys for sale upon their rusting Ford,
and nothing cost more than seventy-five cents.
And nothing was sold from 9 A.M. to noon.
And one of the children found a dead snake

in a nearby ditch and brought it to Ma,
who said they couldn't cook it for lunch.
Who said they'd have Kool Aid and corn.
Who sent the oldest daughters down the road
to beg several ears of corn from a farm

as the father pretended he didn't hear.
As a crow picked at the discarded snake.
As the oldest son picked up a rock,
the father touched his arm, shook his head
and grinned; took a rifle from the trunk.

And the mother felt her marrow shiver.
And the crow flew up with half a snake,
which swayed like a question mark's curve
—with the snake's bit head as its dot.
The father's shots missed; the crow rose

and an invisible question crossed fields.
The bullets hit neither girl: they hit corn
five yards away. Some ears jumped apart
from stalks as the girls stared in awe.
The girls thanked God and gathered corn.

The mother tasted dead snake till dark.

Earthling

I'm thinking again of a man on the roof of a small cheap hotel. He lives below and no longer works. His family is gone away. Cinders, broken glass, pigeon feathers, tennis ball, a spoon. . . . Just before sunrise. He looks at his left palm and looks at the right. He knows no place in this city where eyes would look at them and try to understand. The sun's pink blush, and now its orange glow. The hands played ballgames. They turned pages and wrote and touched a girl's cheek. Touched breasts and went to war, where they touched blood. Eyes in places like bars would glaze with indifference or turn away. His fingers and palms carrying a lunchpail, moving tools and machines, tousling a child's hair. Touched by *cold*, by gifts, by tears. The glow now so deeply orange it is also crimson, and the sun visible between an office building and warehouse. And the man having to squint as he faces that way. The sun like a vast, unblinking eye whose gaze he feels on both palms. They once pushed against the shoulders of a woman giving birth. The man holds them toward the sun. They once slapped a friend, hauled a dead enemy, held a snake, held telephones, railings, cupcakes. . . .

Siblings

Woman on a downtown street
begging passers-by for a name. "Any
name—please," she says, nods as if
to prime your response. "*Please*. May be
the one I lost—" And you shrug;
or you say, "Annamarie" or hold
out a quarter, which she ignores, or:
"Madonna" . . . "Wicked Witch, East"
. . . "Madame Bovary." She frowns,
moves it back, forth; glares
past or through you. "Name, name!
Say a *name*, please." Some people,
women mostly, say their own; then
blush or inhale hard as though to
draw it back. As though the woman's
grin, eyes clearing, would leave
them nameless. You have passed her
often; you've heard a man with
attache case, $300 shoes, murmur
his name a few strides past . . .
just to be sure. You've watched
a teenage girl with eye pupils
like crooked pits yell, "Take
mine, bitch! Laurel. Laurel. . . .
Take it to my old man in hell!"
You've flinched, but she didn't; you
have gone back and stood there:
"Emma. Karla with a K. Paula,
Pearl, Polly—" You have named
every girl or woman you ever loved.
She's frowned, looked through or past
you at calls of "Haggle-tooth" . . . "Lois

Lane" . . . "Margarita." One man
handed you a dollar; a legless
one in fatigue cap said, "Khe
Sanh" and spelled it out. And
wheels himself there daily, where
you and she stand waiting. "Nel,"
you say softly, "Nora, Nana, Nada."
"K-H-E," he calls. Today a man
in silk tie stood watching, began
to cry. "Linda," he said. "Linda,
I'm sorry." She shook her head.
"Linda," he stood repeating. You
heard someone behind read from
an obituary page. A city bus paused;
from its doors and windows mouths
leaned and widened, widened. You
shook your head. Their voices shook
you. "Mustang Sally" . . . "H-I-V,"
"Zsa-Zsa" . . . "Mama." Then sirens
rose, named you all, and vanished.

Fireman's Story

"I brought out the 7-year-old.
Dead—just dead. They all
were in a bedroom, dresser
pushed to a window. The 8-

year-old, the 6. The 4, two
2-year-olds. Rolanda, 7 months.
I put him down, Ali; didn't
know his name then. Didn't

know boy or girl. Some of
the burnt flesh on my gloves,
rubber coat. . . . Placed him,
it, with the others and ran

—I ran to that mother's
eyes. *'You bitch!'* I opened
my mouth to shriek. Seven
kids alone with barred windows

against thieves. I wanted to
rub my gloves in her face.
Her face was dead. I mean,
was stark numb pain; it

stopped me, and I puked.
Her eyes were windows without
bars . . . and in them she
was 7 years old. She was 9,

and 6. Left alone. Alone
at 2 and 22 with no way out.
Never. Do you understand?
Fuck it. She was younger

and older than you'll ever
be. Went out for a drink;
I mean, she lived behind
bars with seven kids. She

slipped between them for one
hour—there were witnesses.
I stood there with burnt
flesh and puke on my coat.

She never saw me. Seven
kids inside her, and wide
eyes not wide enough for us
to even get out Rolanda."

City

A small black boy in Chicago wakes up and finds he cannot see. He shouts for his mother. He shrieks for her. A frail old white woman in Chicago sings an Irish ballad so tenderly she begins to cry. She nods at a photograph and smiles.

The boy's mother runs into his bedroom and holds him. He had seen his friend's head fly apart from bullets the day before. In school—the class was learning about Antarctica. That word is the answer to an item in the crossword puzzle the old woman will work on this afternoon.

The mother sits on her son's bed and rocks him, rocks him. Her eyes are closed. The old woman moves to a phone and dials a precinct. She closes her eyes at her son's voice, and for some instants the face in the photograph is alive again. A whiskey-like warmth enters her that will last until noon.

She doesn't hear her son's words because she is thanking God for her life. Her son doesn't hear them because he is thinking about whiskey. It is too early in the day, far too early, so he thinks about his daughter's face. On the desk in front of him are photographs of a small corpse, but the detective sees an older girl with auburn hair.

He sees her dressed for First Communion. The daughter is now a nurse, and she is dressing again in white that will make faces of the adults and children she will touch this day seem an even richer, lovelier brown than they are.

The boy being rocked now on his bed forms the word "Antarctica"—and his mother holds him tighter.

The Years

Small pale man enters an old hotel
and turns slow circles in its lobby.
Each takes a few minutes, and when
asked, the man says: "A year. Each

time around is one year. Since she
and I stayed here. " The security
man has to keep moving polished shoes
to face him. The two appear

to be waltzing—and one young boy
nudges his younger sister and points
at them. And they giggle. The small
pale man suddenly stops, nods once

at the man in front of him; he
raises hands palm-upward as though
in a shrug. Or as though holding,
or wishing to hold, many years.

And he leaves. His reflection
leaves the polished shoes, which
continue turning their human weight.
The boy stops smiling. His sister turns.

An August

Meanwhile, a teenage boy knows a way
to the roof of an abandoned building
in the South Side. And he goes there
at night, alone; he sits on cinders
above graffiti and lean cats and sirens
and under the moon. He has no

guitar or saxophone, so his brown
fingers move the ballcap he wears
sideways everyplace else. There he puts
it on his lap and listens to what
the night and his pulse say . . . then
his fingers make the cap say it

in his mind. When this music
grows most hopeful reaching toward
lights high in housing projects,
he has an erection. When the moon
is near full and the sky is clear,
the boy's fingernails gleam it.

This Morning

Behind all these poems are three
worn people entering a McDonald's
in 1995. It could be Hardee's—
It could be a man alone, wife
and child two or several states
away and inside him. Could be
a woman, black, eyes hard forever
at stains of blood and vomit, piss
and raped childhood passed between
a housing project and grade school.
But say this thin white family:
man shaved yesterday but not today;
woman has rinsed her hair auburn
but not recently; their boy's hungry.
Their boy is hungry. The three don't
touch, but you can feel touching
between them. You guess they slept
in a car last night and soon
will sell it. Or abandon it flat-
out empty of gas or brake linings
—and the radio they'll sell for
the last pizza they'll have delivered.
I don't know. What do I know . . .
have delivered to a dumpster? Eyes
hard as glass fragments around them
while they toast one another and laugh,
crush beer and pop cans with fingers.
Next day they'll search the dumpster
for half-Big Macs and pizza crusts.
Today I want them somehow present
in each poem. In that McDonald's
they can afford the brief respite

from the weather, the slight dignity
of standing there gazing at prices.
The boy—say he is twelve—knows
what they are better than he does
a home phone number. His mother
and father will get angry enough
to slap him if what he orders
doesn't cost the difference between
their coffees and the five dollars
in the man's pocket. The boy grits
teeth and fights down nausea at
how both their stares will avoid
his Sausage Egg McMuffin and fries
. . . how he'll push half the fries
at them and risk a slap. The man
has a mustache the woman saw one
night fifteen years ago and knew,
knew, she had to touch. She rose
near orgasm soon after at its first
caressing her navel. Now she barely
notices it beneath the abyss
of his eye pupils, and he hates either
himself or her at the cheapening look
of her hair. At each curve of her
face or body seeming a sharp edge,
each sound of her voice. "Luck,"
is what they said a lot at first:
"bad luck," then "shitty" or "fucking-
goddam" . . . then no longer used
the word as they moved farther away
from the closed factory. The yard sale.
And then the second and third yard

sale, the one the man and woman
cried at and wouldn't come inside
from the rain to the empty flat—
though the boy stood in the doorway
begging them to. That yard sale
is not far behind any of these poems
about my country that are true.
How they stopped crying, and drove
from that address and haven't cried
since. The boy hates it that they
no longer cry, and he can't. Soon
his coldest fear may be realized
as the man leaves them or doesn't.
Doesn't, and lashes out the rage
the boy feels behind the mustache,
the woman feels now on her nape
as the three move to the counter. No
one behind it will say, "Have a good
day." The black or Latino teen
working there for minimum wage may
start to, but will stop. And there
between these four beings and four
unspoken words will hover so much
fierce courage and tender, coiled
fury that eight eyes will lower
as from a mirror shouting: "Help!"

Man with Baseball Mitt
Outside Wrigley Field

He has caught balls hit over the left-field wall during batting practice. He doesn't know that what he yearns to catch is a yellow bird, then let it go. His father used to catch fish off Puerto Rico. He has an older sister who once caught syphilis. She went to a doctor and was cured.

He has a son he's never seen who will be caught stealing candy bars from a convenience store at age seven. This will make an indelible imprint, the boy believing himself terminally inept at crime. He will go to Wrigley Field years later and see a slim man among the teenagers with mitts and ballcaps across Waveland Avenue from left field.

The man will leap and catch a ball that would have hit a brick apartment building. To the boy it will appear as though the ball changed shape, turned yellow and feathered, just before its smack into the mitt. The boy will later write and perform songs, and the one that will make many people know his name for a brief period will be about a man who catches yellow birds, then lets them go.

The man will keep coming to Waveland Avenue long after he is too old to outjump or outscramble teenage boys there for baseballs. After his final afternoon trying, he will catch a bus and travel through a cold October rain to a boarding house on the northwest side. He will think, climbing steps with his worn, lovingly oiled mitt under his shirt to protect it, of his father once turning to him and seeming to smile twice as wide as his wide mustache.

The father later disappeared with his small yellow boat in a storm that caught many people along that coast unaware. The time he smiled so broadly, then laughed like the glitter of sun on the Caribbean, the son who would grow old in Chicago had asked why he whistled each time he cast his line from the boat. "Each fish I want has a small bird inside," the father said. "The birds like music and will steer the fish this way. . . ."

A Chicago

Tonight, Friday night, a woman
there will put on a wide, snap-brim
1940's style hat. Say dark green.
Say she's forty-five years old, lives
alone and has twenty dollars to spend
if she skips lunch Monday and Tuesday.
Hasn't had a cigarette since Sunday,
after church Sunday. "Went to St. Whosis,"
she told a co-worker, " 'cause it was *there.*
In the neighborhood. Liked I couldn't
understand a word." The co-worker chewed
gum in reply. Tonight under the hat
tilted at a rakish angle—"Rakish,"
the woman will murmur to her mirror—
her irises' color will look "worn"
to her. She will shrug. She will
give her mirror the finger. Baring
her teeth in a smile, she will move
as though to music on high heels from
her two-room apartment to the street.
Black blouse, black skirt less tight
at the waist last time out. Suede
vest, gold. "Dirty gold," she'd told
the co-worker after buying it. "Prob'ly
never wear it, but what the hell?
You know?" Now she wears it, wears
earrings the color of gold, two inch-
long question marks. Wears a necklace
with a small jade dragon. It sways
between her breasts as she walks.
She carries a purse, and in the purse
is a can of mace. She knows how

to use it because she did once.
Say she walks a block and walks
another block. She waits for a bus.
Say she waits for a bus, whistling
very softly and off-key "I Can't
Believe That You're in Love with Me,"
which I heard one night and felt
so close to my spine I knew my
marriage would have to change or end.
Say this woman was once married.
Say the sky is now the velvet,
near-dusk blue it was on a beach
I walked haunted by the song: I
yearned to be *in love* again. Say
the moon is nearly full, and see it
seem balanced on the woman's snap-
brim dark green hat. She is very
brave right now, and that and the hat
and her hazel eyes and small shadows
at her mouth-corners moving as she
says, "What the hell? Nobody's perfect"
make her beautiful. She will ride
the bus to meet in a restaurant a man
she's never seen. He answered her ad
under "Personals" and is moving now
toward her with everything he is.

"Creative Writing"

The mother felt her twelve-year-old's
eyes as she stepped from the bathtub.
Two doors between them were ajar—
he'd thought he was alone upstairs
and could search his father's trousers
for coins. He'd thought he might look
again at condoms in his father's drawer.
The mother felt her son's breath halt
in his throat at her gleam of firm
breasts, at her pubic hair and blush.
She *felt* it. The boy stepped backward
from the drawer—which also held, he
suddenly remembered, the belt his father
used for spankings. His gaze and hers
seemed loud through the house. Then
they both shrugged, and it was the first
time he'd ever done that; and hers moved
breasts in a way that never quite stopped
inside the boy. He grew into a man
with few male friends and many words
for how splendor is touched by eyes.

"Only the Valiant—"

Two farm wives in middle age
walking together daily for exercise
fall in love. They acknowledge this
by both pointing out some geese
flying the wrong way—bumping hands
and lowering them clasped. And
releasing them as the mailman's Ford
rises over the gravel slope ahead.
Two women in a son's and husband's
bulky ex-jackets who had *laughed*
at sons and husbands, at themselves,
at fools in a garage-sale novel
one loaned the other . . . two women
in sons' ex-Nikes bumping jacket
sleeves three more times that day.
Each time strums them. Each grins
that evening at Monday Night Football
games they hate. Each rises Tuesday
with an image of geese flying
toward a gray *cold* lean of time.
Flying, though, not inert: not alone.

Exuberance

There was a cook standing beside a river through an old city where two barges were passing. The cook's eyes met a woman's on the farther barge from him, and the cook felt pierced from his childhood to future aging. His cells glowing, the cook leaped onto the nearer barge—but of course the eyes faded all the faster, faded smaller than the period ending this sentence.

And on the barge where he now stood was a man drunk with wine beating his son with language. The cook made him stop, touched the boy's tears with a finger and touched it to the father's lips. Meanwhile, he knew his life would contain less joy than his capacity for it because two lustrous eyes had entered him and gone away.

So he stayed on the father's barge, since it didn't matter where he was, and when they came to a port, the cook shrugged and said goodbye. The boy cried again; the cook carried the warmth of tears in his fingers to a bakery, where he was hired. One day he saw from its window the woman passing again on the barge—but her eyes were different now, only lovely, and he did not stop kneading dough to run after them.

And he didn't have a tear fall into the dough. His fingers moved the glow and taste of joy, of tears, into breads and pastries and muffins that entered children's cells in that port. When the children went outside, when they traveled or moved away, their eyes gave a luster to roofs and barges and trees and roads that never quite faded.

The Words

Do young men now wear ballcaps backward
because they are afraid of the future?
When I was young. . . . *When I was*
young—a phrase so sweet it hurts,
my friends and I explored used bookstores.
Tyler and Ken and I, and maybe Arno.
And Ken is dead. We made fun of him

in our ballgames for combing his hair
between innings. I'm trying to discover
what I want to say here. When I
was young, the future was an alcove
in a used bookstore where nobody seemed
to have pulled a bulb's cord for months,
and Ken or Tyler or I pulled it. *"What*

you kids doin' back there!" And saw past
the alcove another alcove full of books!
Tyler wanted Nero Wolfs. I'd tingle
from eyes to navel at "P. G. Wodehouse"
on a book's spine. Ken came to be with us.
I miss my friends so much this morning

I want to cry. Do I remember once putting
a bulb in an empty socket of that inner
alcove? *"You kids leave things like you*
find them, hear me!" We left them better:
straight piles beside piles on the floor,
spines all turned outward on shelves.
We were in love. It's a love story. Ken

died years later—and when I learned
about that, I felt: but he was only
a boy. . . . *He was just a young boy.*
He never wore a ballcap. He came along
to the bookstores to help us laugh,
make faces toward the unshaven man in front—

the fool who didn't know there was nothing
you couldn't hope for in this world.
Nothing. Where you pull a small cord,
and Ken's hair and all the words *gleam.*

Fragment in Us

A woman lies on her side
between two humans who lie between
two more. . . . They press together
because of a chain; they bend
slightly at the waist and knees.

They sway with the ship and ocean,
and they sweat. They would glisten
if above them a rectangle of dark
moved and light touched them.
But it doesn't move; wood groans

and they do. The woman's navel
is hard against the curved spine
of a woman from another tribe
who died six hours ago. Spoons:
they are packed like spoons from

Africa to Virginia, and now she
cries out, and the scalding dark
pins of air pierce harder at
temples . . . arteries. Her navel
jitters against the corpse, heaves

and the corpse's weight is firm,
is firm. The woman has a name,
but no one in the instants
around her knows it. Writhing,
she howls, throbs; she gives birth.

Tunnel Rat on the Dance Floor

grinning with the medic
who'd told me, "Burn victims
were the worst"—because you can
only give them so much morphine
without killing them,

and because they *scream*.
And if twenty years
weren't long enough to bury
those echoes, a small man who
crawled in tunnels

and now stands grinning
at blues poured down
from a bandstand helps. You
both moved an inch, a half-
inch at a time

when you were young
and more alive than now—
with gauze at an aid station,
with flashlight in the earth.
Nothing will give

you back those inches;
but sometimes a few guitars,
keyboard and drum and another
vet's eyes can teach them
how to dance.

—for Dick Ihlenfeld

Gulf Legs

I have an image of someone
dancing on the roof of a hospital,
veterans' hospital, under the moon.
Someone? It's a young black man
without legs from one of the beds
inside. His legs and feet exist now
only as bone fragments in Iraq. . . .
And as photographs and memories, and
dreams. In some dreams he dances.
In some dreams he leaps to release
a jump shot so perfect it becomes
the moon. And when he lands
on the roof and seems to plunge
through it up to his thighs—
which smack cinders there so hard
the moon turns red—and when his
testicles do and his penis, navel,
palms, nipples, his lips press
cinders until dawn . . . the moon
cools to become two scar-tissued
ovals of stumps. And he's awake
in a ward. In southern Iraq
a piece of bone small as a tear
glows under the moon. In a park
in the soldier's hometown, fragments
of bottles and crack vials reflect
a sunrise the color of rust under
netless rims. Toes and ankles, knees
writhe under housing-project sheets
at gunshots below. In one dream
there, the guns aren't a gang's—
or a cop's, or despair- or wine-

or crack-insane neighbor's: they are
an enemy's half the world away.
The dreamer dreams starched, clean
desert camouflage fatigues; he
moves in boots with such grace
toward the enemy it seems like
dancing. . . . And in the image I
have now, there are musicians
around the sweat-rank mattress
he shares with a brother; there
is a bandleader in corporate
executive suit, his waxed shoes
glowing like full moons.

English Instructor Begins
Summer Vacation

Straightened out, all the commas
I have placed in red on students' themes
would reach from here to the heart
of a woman named Red. I just
decided that; she will sleep later
than usual this morning. Once Red
was a student in Freshman English
and wrote half a theme: *"Topic*
is why come to college what do
I want out of life? How about
money fun and sex; just kidding.
I want love. Kids maybe. Some-
thing to do that means something.
Hey I want to dye my hair red as
blood & make sad people smile,
you dig?" And she added a few
more sentences and went out for beers,
fell in love and got hurt bad,
and quit school. *"Roger you*
sonofa-bitch!" is how the note
began she dropped off at his
fraternity house. Twenty years ago; today
is her birthday, but she has
to work. She once had a job
as an exotic dancer. She'd run
out of money in Phoenix and agreed
to sway G-string and breasts
with stars covering nipples as long
as no one touched her. When
the owner did, she kicked him
in the balls so hard—it

was late and they were alone
in the club—she had to take him
to the hospital. It was that night,
packing again, she came upon
her half-theme in a notebook.
This afternoon and evening, Red
will touch and joke with people
in wheelchairs, wearing diapers
and tubes. In Phoenix she laughed
at her sentences and then cried.
She added a few commas; she
stayed awake until dawn gazing
at white space following her words
with its blue lines like prison
bars. And then she turned
the notebook sideways, and she
scrawled: *"In one year I'll be
a redhead & a practical nurse!!"*
And she was. Later she was briefly
married, but that's another story.
This one is about the invisible red
arc between these words and an ex-
student I'm imagining with hair
more vivid than all my commas,
my "RO's" for run-on sentences—
With eyebrows arched now in her mirror
as she remembers the date, grins,
leans forward to kiss herself.

Marjorie Trudell

The pond was there, and the sun.
And my father, eighty-four, stunned—
poised, afraid and brave. Small
fiesta on Sunday in a park

in my city. Chris Plata sang
a ballad, and his wife was there
on bass guitar. Another guitar,
drums. My brother was there,
who lives in London. Egg rolls,

fliers against pesticides. Organic
fruits, salads. My mother, eighty-
two, was shriveled in a hospital
between tubes and machines. Grass

and ducks, tennis courts, Spanish
with Chris's rolled R's, and my
mother wet in my eyes. The colors
of T-shirts and food and songs,
Sundays. Laughter. The blonde woman

I love was there. Later told me
she put an arm around my father.
As we walked toward my car,
red, by tennis courts. Their bright

gleams of fencing. The fragrant motes
of air from living things. She
said a tear was there, moving
on his face. Trees. I don't
pray, but I begged my mother

not to leave this earth. Please
not yet become that precious:
transparent as music, as love.

White Horses

A small girl in Buffalo carries
her grandfather's lunch past shops.
And say it is 1918; she didn't
say as she was dying this month.
This morning my mother carries it

and her smile at how *proud*
she feels—she felt in a breathing
mask and tubes and morphine. . . .
Carries the lunch past six white
horses: "Oh they were something!

Everyone knew Captain John Ruch,
and I'd take his lunch from home
to the fire station." And in shops
they watch young Marjorie and know
who she is. The lunch—say it

is kept warm in a basket; she
didn't say in her hospital bed
as we touched her and smiled:
we cried, and will see no fear
at her facing death for the rest

of our lives. . . . Carries lunch
past the firemen who call out
her name and smile, and wave.
Past six horses white as youth,
as hope and seventy-six years

of days ahead. And she goes
once again to Captain John Ruch
with his warm lunch; and he
smiles his mustache so wide
it reaches from then to now.

A January

Father and two sons shooting baskets.
In falling snow, and upon snow
muffling the ball's bounces and their voices.
And their laughter. The smallest boy
feels the snowflakes on flesh as tickles;
he tries shots his brother just tried,
and sometimes makes them. The ball
is speckled as it arcs—then freed
of white by the backboard or rim or net
to gleam again. So to this father
every shot is perfect, and his heart
feels tickled by snowflakes. The older
boy now stands under the chain net,
looking up. Counts aloud how many
flakes drift through the net, but can't
keep up. Opens mouth and points there;
the younger comes over and counts,
and giggles. And he and the father
open mouths—and as I lie dying,
somewhere snowflakes will touch laughter.

Paper Route

My mother is out pruning her petunias.
She is not dead. My father is not
old and alone. I am not bald. It's

morning again if I write that our dog
Friday is beside me with the grass
shimmering dew. My paper route: he
noses worms pressing from separate

holes and what gleams between them.
It's white and scary, and nobody has
to age or die if I chase him from it.
The news is only paper. Tomorrow

it will say something else: the worms
will press again because it is spring.
Friday will nose them because he
is not dead. My brother is not

living in another country. It's white
and scary sometimes before and after
poems, and it's not morning anymore.

& Earlier

I am part of the essential majority. I am one more leaf on the great human tree.

PABLO NERUDA ────────────────────────────

Shawl Defense

Last night Bonnie and I watched a movie on TV about the tiny Indiana school winning the state basketball championship. Devin came home from sitting in street clothes on the sophomore team bench because of mononucleosis. He and I wanted to play; and we have a small hoop taped above the opening to the dining room, and we have a sponge ball. She smiled from her chair and then *smiled* as Devin blocked my double-pump from near the sofa, passed to himself off the wall for a lay-up, then blocked my hesitation hook. Made a jump shot as the crowd roared on TV and Maria the cat changed her mind about crossing the room past us. I switched hands gliding over carpet at age forty-nine and shot wrong-handed under his arms, and it hung there and dropped through. But he stayed longer in the air than I for another jumper and mine hit only plant, and she said we should take it easy.

But Devin didn't, slammed a dunk and laughed as I invented some turnaround thing that bongled off her chair arm, and she laughed. She laughed in her shawl and green bathrobe and her eyes and breasts I'd tasted again that afternoon, and above her fears and a sad dream about her mother waiting in her nerves. Devin had entered this world between her legs, only hers; and there he was larger than a bald friend and husband, blocking shots, grinning the same light as her eyes. Showing us he could take off after two steps from the bedroom and sail through the dining room to lay it in from behind. She agreed to be the defense against him and me; but her first move was to throw the shawl up to smother a shot, which knocked the hoop off the wall. They kidded about the weather on TV as she laughed

and then didn't, and the hoop went to a table for Devin
or me to put back up today. And her eyes were briefly
uncertain, then smiled and *smiled* as I did and her son
did and we hugged her and said goodnight.

1988

Tim Kelly's Eyes

Tim Kelly's eyes, in Mississippi, hearing a second black man singing "Danny Boy" for him from the bottoms of toes that night, at the Elks Club for blacks outside of Greenville: for blacks and civil-rights workers that summer, when Tim came from retirement after San Francisco docks and grappling hooks . . . other fights, wins and losses, to sit near me shining, *shining* through tears at the chorus—at mothers, grandmothers maybe, of the singers up before dawn and out in cotton fields that Friday until sunset, for three dollars, 1964, three dollars a day: sweat along curves of sacred dark flesh gleaming like—*"But come ye back when summer's in the mea-dow"*. . . gleaming like the hard and soft pupils, aged and young, of Tim Kelly s eyes.

Ballad of Jesse Howe

who stood daily in the blue,
blue, not wholly unpoisoned heat
of South Chicago moving two
of the thinnest arms on any kid there

making shot after shot from twenty feet.
The basketball's patch was the color
of bubblegum; and Jesse's
eyes as it wobbled and would have

kissed only net if the rim
had a net, those large bright curves
of *joy*, are what folks later remembered.
They sighed or wailed being

slapped around by fatigue or booze
or despair in the project's
buildings, sweated and bloomed
cancers, as Jesse bounced. He

was simply *always* there: older
kids gave up trying to keep him
out of their games. And soon—
though he seemed too busy

moving that skinny branch of
right arm outside T-shirts stolen
from a laundromat to remember
to grow: still under five feet

in ninth grade, in tenth . . .
soon he always scored more
from where he kept backing out
than any dunker jostling and swearing

up close. "*Do* it, Jesse! " they'd
hear through grease on the third,
the fourth floors—through TV's
and stereos and lead fumes

breathed to and from work,
or from looking for work. Or from
looking for what they had once almost
believed they might be. And it

would complete the arc and
do it, zing through the rusted
hoop once again—the ball and the
balls Jesse kept backing farther

to gleam high above boomboxes,
to push back at the chill
off the lake, to gather flakes of somehow
already dirty falling snow,

on the way to yet another
high bounce under the rim and
"*Shit!*" from the other team. In
Jesse's sixteenth fall, he stood

four feet eleven inches above blacktop
and was said to not have been
within ten feet of the hoop
since his first erection—which

made everything in Jesse grin,
move back a step, yell for the ball.
When he didn't show one day,
it was said he was on the other

side of Building C waiting
to shoot from there; when he didn't
appear for a week, an ex-
teammate high on dust said he was

sighting from a chunk of ice
on the lake, but no one laughed.
When he was found inert
around a switchblade with small

hands grasping at his missing ball
under rubble in a bathtub
of a condemned building, their
eyes turned a little harder. They

moved an invisible few steps
nearer the shriek of wind between
buildings in the project; they
grew up with another, short,

luminous-eyed reason to jab
something sharp at someone clutching
what they didn't own. And grew
far, far away from practicing

a turnaround, double-pump dunk;
and only a few—maybe one
every year—heard. *"Do* it, Jesse!"
in the wind or a pulse.

The Window

He was a sick child,
light was fragile for him, in him:
and he sat at a window
watching the others making grass and sky more vivid
with their running their voices—

They never looked his way—
as he never gathered his strength
and opened the window, and called:
"You in the red sweater, you cheated!
You never tagged the girl
who owns the dog with the one brown ear!"

"Okay," they never shouted back;
"Thank you—" His eyes grew large,
grew luminous from what he did not say.
His sickness failed, then died, and he moved timidly
out onto grass and breathed.

The others felt more vivid
near his eyes, their games felt more wild;
they taught him the rules, although
he already knew. And he laughed
the last shreds of sickness
from the trees. And his eyes

became healthy and lost some light.
The other children forgot the dark glow
in their marrow from his gaze as they
loved him and fought him: and all
the children grew and went away

from a window that often reflected the sun.

Music

Jack, I remember
how you and the other kids
poured down that long slide
    and out of childhood
in the dusk, at the picnic that June

and I'm crying now
at eight-thirty in the morning
because your laughter slowed, voices
    grew thinner than the light
on grass, on leaves, brick, T-shirts

and still you came, and stood, and
climbed up to do it again
and again . . . flowing and bounce
    of hair, luster of eyes, rump-
halves like denim apples slanting

toward where we stood, singing
you in our veins, singing goodbye
for you and to you and wanting time
    to keep pouring one gift
after another in return for our deaths.

Nicaraguan Village

The rain that falls on poverty
is a sound saying hearts do not break,
they absorb. After the rain
the raw sun inside stomachs will brighten the village.
The one above will beckon the hunger,
the headaches: *Come, Grow.* . . .
Colors will shriek as they lean their mute boredom,
boredom. Or it will rain all day.
Or an old woman will hear the drumming
on the tin shacks long after it stops,
and then will die. Or a child
will grow weaker and feel like the rain,
the solid piss of it from a drainspout.
And the pig without a reflection,
and the pink sheen that it drinks from
between a shack and a shack—like diluted blood,
like watered wine, like the flesh
of suburban U.S. babies. . . .
And the tears of trees around the village. . . .
And the eyes hidden from sight in the dawn
where no one walks, where a lone pig changes color
and the road goes in four directions—
and the road goes in four directions like a crude
stick-drawing of a crucifixion. . . .
And the end of these sentences is in the capital.
No, it is inside the eyes, in the breasts,
in the rain that will fall the next day or the blaze of heat.
The stones along the road,
between the road and the shacks:
like people huddled together because they are alive and conscious,
because their hearts beat louder in a crowd.

If It Dies

Managua, 1979

I am thinking about how purely
a young man's hand fits onto his wrist—
and the flow of wrist, forearm, elbow. . . .
How lovely. And the curvatures,
muscle and tissue and veins softening
dusk to amber on a right arm, say,
holding a pistol. On the street of a city.

The light muted by smoke of unnatural things burning;
tires, plastic . . . the smell. The arm
rises to slope abruptly at "shoulder"
in English. And the shirt which smells
like Central America, like Chicago
on a pleasant September evening
with the housing projects rising like *mañana*.

A small pistol, for instance;
no larger than the hand or a piece of fruit—
and how complex and innocent
the biology in each finger.
I am counting lines. Seven for each
stanza. The constant rub
of human flesh along time and possibility.

The swim. You are not in love
with your own or anyone else's arm
right now, probably. As the softest
rest for your gaze against the chatter
of weapons and sheen of worn streets
In a city I pronounce incorrectly.
The way one day becomes another

like a voice entering and leaving
words. A young man's arm leaving and entering
in a sleeve of a shirt. We say
"shirt." They say—something else.
They crouch there in the streets against
my fear of disorder. Against our burden
of "class." As the arm dies,

if it dies, something like the shape
of fingers into palm and wrist
and forearm into elbow—we call it
"elbow"—snaps between your eyes,
my eyes, and the luminous fruit
of our brains. Snaps forever. And yet
here is another. And another. Another. . . .

A Checkered Red and White Shirt

I am looking at a picture
of two children lying on a floor
in Central America.
There is blood on the floor,
there is blood on the children.
One is looking toward the other
and seems to see him. I
want to give them to you
and to keep the children.
I want to be worthy of the pale
gold and orange light around
and from their bodies. It
will not happen here or now.

The second one sees nothing,
or very little. And this:
some gauze beside his mouth
is the brightest thing in sight
and seems his final vapor
escaping. His hands are fists.
His left leg is tilted wrong.
There is an adult hand
on his stomach, there is an adult
weight pulling my eyes.
His brother — now I believe
the two are brothers—
has a large navel. He died too,
soon afterward, the caption says.

He died too. The hand went away.
My eyes will go away. Somoza
went away, and Duarte did too.
Montt came and killed, and left.
Mexico and Honduras and Lubbock,
Texas. . . . I don't know.
If these children's providers
had not been made desperate enough
to fight, the boys would
probably be alive now.
Perhaps lying hungry on an
unsmeared floor. Perhaps
riding in a truck to join
the Guard. Perhaps watching
the arc of a piece of fruit
connect their hands.

This poem will not end,
it will stop. Quit. Two boys
on a floor now washed clean.
Or bombed to fragments.
They were born and lived
and then came to this picture.
The one hurrying nowhere else,
the younger one, has a shirt
on the other side of his skull
from the gauze. As though
someone put it there as a pillow
he couldn't stay on. Or as though
he had hugged it like a mother
and then stopped hugging.

The Artists

I leaned a box of crayons
against a shack where people lived,
and backed away. It was morning;
the box was small and it grew smaller

in the dirt, in Nicaragua, leaning
on a door without paint, a home
without windows or a toilet or sink
or a coloring book. Or a floor—

the dirt beneath me was the dirt
beneath the family I would never see.
And it was so quiet; even the rooster's
cries were absorbed there like water,

like tears or sweat, or blood. And kids
used the crayons and now they're gone:
the green maybe trees for that treeless street,
the yellow a new box of crayons.

Isthmus

I have one way to imagine
the poverty in those countries:
A son goes off to join the rebels,
or is seen talking with a girl
whose brother is suspected of having
listened to some students who later
may have become rebels. . . . And the son
is killed—one evening cut in half,
and morning is three friends holding his mother
from two directions she must not go.
Three hungry women gripping the loud
grief and thin arms of their town
as a woman, of their country as hell-
wild and tear-pasted strands of hair
against cheeks and their bone. . . .
And gripping their neighbor, whose name
they know, whose child they had fed;
and the shack among the shacks
shrieks his name, and God's, as the town
murmurs their names. So the box
comes from two directions—and the priest
takes a chance and comes, and it
goes into the ground, half her soul.
The son was sixteen and had
his picture taken once. This is where
the poverty moves in me. The children
from haciendas are also portraits in frames
of starting school, of First Communions,
soccer teams, formal dances . . . slides
of grinning in opulent, bizarre lobbies
at Miami Beach, films of diving-board
antics at a U. S. fraternity, of grandchildren

refusing to smile, to stand still, in new
clothing—holding their Bibles. The parents
watch these with the glow from projector bulbs
on the soft, tiny hairs along faces—
to the tinkle of ice cubes and amusement
of friends. Around them the walls are higher
than last year, and they run the images
backward and *laugh* at the blue,
Caucasian-blue-eyed, water unsplashing
a grinning young, nose-holding man to a board.
In a shack a woman will stare at the new
glaze of distance that one afternoon
seems to cover the small picture she holds.
She is careful—but has she touched it
too often? Her son had it taken by a machine
in the capital city: he did that instead
of eating two meals. And now . . . has she
looked there too often? The face
is the same, but are faded tears pulling
her sight after them? She must put
it away, and she will, and knows
she will touch it again the next day.
One picture. Does the light make it dull?
Do her eyes? Does the blackness under
the dirt where she sits when the soldiers
come to search? She is careful—but the water
is scarce, and she cannot clean
her hands every time and cannot not
touch the face each day. She touches
it. The air is mute. The camera
was in a booth whose flattened walls are now
part of a home for a dozen people.

We All Came Out . . .

We all came out to watch.
They showed us how fast
a killer could fly, how *loud*.
They ripped an hour of summer.
We were on their side;
under my irony, something didn't mind
my sons wanting more,
more. In Southeast Asia
that shriek over the trees
was a knife in children's eyes,
death grinning the sky.
In our park two miles
from the airport, the grass
was greener as they passed.
They spread, and almost touched;
I ate my hot dog;
they skimmed the curve of our gaze
again, and again. Air show.
The bombing continues this week
in another poor country.
The sky slamming into the earth,
the earth slamming back. God
and the light opening seeds
receded into whatever the old
and young clutch as sanity explodes—
perhaps each other. Now.
I wiped my mouth
with a napkin; on the climbing bars
beside me were a dozen young pilots.
They moved at the speed of late afternoon
toward brown children in huts and caves.
They spread around the park.

They touched, and ran and stopped.
The blade of the sky was wiped clean
for awhile. I washed dishes.
My sons stayed up late that night
to watch the earth's shadow
replace the moon.

1981

Green Tomatoes

Our eye pupils are always honest.
Death is the eye pupils
widening until that's all there is. Even the future,
even that young girl in the purple jersey
and a psychiatrist worried about tomorrow, even the eel
my son thought he saw in our lake,
will vanish like last week's
circumference of green tomatoes.
All this movement around me is a flow toward death.
Therefore, many feel
they must regard time like a trough.
But if death is an explosion of all our cells,
eh?—if death is an explosion outward
to join the cosmos, like an idea
tentacles outward in all directions from its source
in a human brain, and a mouth moves,
a hand reaches out, cautiously,
or sailing like a fat gull,
like a porpoise, toward a breast or holster. . . .
Eh? If death is a shoehorn
and everything we don't know is the foot. . . .
Or a fulcrum—death is where we
finally balance history and birth.
I'm sitting in a drugstore coffee shop
trying to write a revolutionary poem.
But old people keep getting older, rolled-up sleeves
keep passing nearby, keep fading
whether I can see it or not, keep straining
to weave air between their threads, to become dust.
And now that old woman with hair like a dead shirt
has said my name, has asked me
between its letters
if she is still alive. . . .

The Light in Our Bodies

After supper the children go out to play.
It is a holy truth.
Notice I did not say, "After supper
we go out to play."
We went out to play, as we walked

back and forth to school,
full of the light in our bodies—
which the adult world didn't know
what to do with.
Having lost their own,
they became teachers or irrelevant

to us behind their newspapers.
My parents' love
was as holy as hide-and-seek,
but I couldn't *play* with it.
So I cleaned my plate and ran away,

and came to this place where every night
after supper, the children go outside. . . .

Father

I have been learning what the word means
for ten years now. No, for thirty-nine.
My father built me a cardboard fort:
I remember a cloud . . . cardboard clouds. . . .
We each have two sons; we each
have a mustache. When my first son was born,
I stayed awake all night, smoking.
When he learned to talk, I grew a mustache.
When he learned to read, I looked
at my father and saw a gray hawk the size
of a cathedral behind his eyes, sulking.

The bird has flapped wings and dug in talons,
glazing my father's eyes, twice now
in my presence. My younger son can read.
After he was born, I quit a career,
and this morning I have a chill of fear
that I may waste my life. My father
retired five months before I first
saw his eyes glaze over; he didn't
know where he was, but it hurt.
He didn't want to be there; he looked
around the room, mumbling about past mistakes.
My brother and I held him; it was Christmas Eve,
and our children played happily under the tree.

Now my father has moved to this city.
What was it I had to give him . . . ?
I painted streets on a broad rectangle
of wallboard one Christmas for my first son.
He still plays with it. He has seen me
smoke marijuana. . . . He said I know
what you guys were doing in there,
you were mating. *Mating.* I say
"fuck" in front of my parents, who need me too much
to let forms of speech our two generations
were allowed to come between us.

My father had a world war to win,
and he did. He drew airplanes
that flew in the real, unmargined sky.
My younger son loves him. My older
son loves him and has other things to do
than think much about either of us.
The gray hawk still hovers there,
between the halves of my father's heart.
In one of them he is a little boy
again. He is wondering what this
onslaught of time is all about.
He is looking around for his father.
Last night my older son stayed overnight
in another town; I doubt that he missed me.

A Small Black Album

My mother ready for the future
at Angola Beach, south of Buffalo,
sixty-five years ago. I know she's ready
because of her erect little torso
as she sits, and the firm-ripe
flesh around her smile—and the smile,
not mirthful but pleased, assured,
in the warmth on a beach
and the glint from the sun
on her lower lip. . . . She squints
and looks older than she was,
her hands as two fists
in the sand beside her thighs;
her four buttons down the front
of her playsuit or swimsuit, whatever; toes
vulnerable, with the right bare leg
crossed over the left bare leg,
like the companion beside her. And she sits,
erect, body and head leaning slightly
away from her companion—and I am sitting here
alone again trying to write what I feel.
Trying to shine it into the future.
Her arms are thin; her arms are
slim and lovely against the sand
and the sixty-five years between them
and my eyes this morning. Her hair
cut short, bottom-halves of ears naked
to the photographer's words and the shutter—
click!—she wasn't afraid of. Nor of anything
else: the possible wind her arms
are ready for, the gravity beneath
her fists, the husband and two sons

who would move between her thighs.
The tilt of her head and firm
most-of-a-smile and the gently
fierce intelligence visible behind her
eyes and forehead. . . . It would
buffet and hurt, her life—as though
she sensed it would bite harder
than the light on a summer beach;
but not shatter one who knew,
felt from the gleam in her hair
to the trust extending from each toe,
who she was. A small girl alive.
Marjorie Noe. Angola, New York; with time
and her face moving against one
another just about—in the sound
of the lake and the girl's breathing
beside her—just about as quickly
and bright, as dangerous and
calm, as she had wakened that day
expecting. . . . I will end this poem
when I want to; and in the round
seed and face in this photograph
is a certainty that when the camera
was lowered the two girls turned
to their play, my mother decided
what to play. She looks even
brave enough to contain the loneliness
and disappointment such control
would bring. After each sprint
and walk of words against the silence
in paper is the silence in paper,
in the eyes of distant strangers.

Watch Them Die

Our brothers and mothers and cousins with strangers
        between their syllables,
with time leaking out of their genitals. Our neighbors
with trouble filling their plates, with our uncles
and our favorite bus drivers
calling to us in our dreams, bringing
their parents' malignant cysts to our Thursdays, to pre-
        menstrual depressions.
And our birthdays passing too quickly, like shuffled
        cards;
our summers tilting the lakes inside us, emptying them
into the lovely arc
between the seas and the sky, the sky and seas
replenished and cleansed by the rivulets of dead kidneys
        and spleens,
of broken houses, colors of rugs, of picture puzzles, of
        wedding dresses. . . .
Our sisters and their fathers and their brothers and the
        strangers in their sweat
in factories producing the gears for our comforts,
and the poor standing in line for their names,
and the mother-in-law arriving, again without warning,
with her gift-wrapped box of loneliness—   .
joining the horizontal totem pole outside our walls,
the pole of faces we can't turn away from,
the faces that know they have the right
to ask us to watch them die.

The Art of Poetry

You can say anything.
That a young marine charging up a sand incline at Saipan
suddenly thought of mittens on a string.
That after hours in the museum
all is quiet: the Rubens in Trafalgar Square,
for example, stay well within their frames.
That the lake of the mind no longer at civil war
must be lovely and quiet, with delightful small fish
nibbling near the surface.
That Rasputin's toenails
must have been clipped by someone:
where are such traces now?
That the impossible sea
is heaving tonight at the flanks
of a ship with lights and music . . .
of many ships, carrying an unguessable number
of indiscretions, and not a few smokers
considering the jump.
That a flagpole doesn't care—
how silly to march past it on a fine Tuesday
in a small group dressed the same
and hitting the left feet at approximately the same instant.
That the air above your sleeping son's head
is as holy as rain.
That nothing is perfect: an unpleasant woman
said on television tonight I should think of my stink.
That the next person you turn to
may be the only one you'll ever have a chance
to love more than yourself.
That a statue is not a fiesta.

That the snow makes so little noise.
That a car goes by. Slows down, stops, backs up.
Pauses, the motor whirring—and drives off.
It is midnight and October in America.
The small towns are left to the leaves.

The Guest

If one day you are walking along
and suddenly decide to ring the bell
of a lower left flat near the center
of the city, and you do, and a woman
in a paisley housedress answers, asks
what you want and you can't think of
anything to say, just stand there
until finally she smiles, says you
must be Margie's friend and Margie
ain't home yet from whatchacallit,
beauty school, come inside and wait,
and you walk into a coffiny parlor,
nod at a chairbound old crone who
smells like wet carpets, sit paging
Life for May 7, 1963, and listening
to the paisley woman wondering from
the kitchen whether you've ate yet
and enjoy sauerkraut—and as you
say no you haven't and yes you do,
although you hate it, the door opens
and a young woman with improbably
colored hair, gum, and a rather nice
figure comes in, says hi, and you say
hi and start to introduce yourself
when you hear the housedress coming,
ask instead to use the bathroom,
and follow the shrug and forefinger
into the dining room (nodding at
the paisley on the way), then duck
into the kitchen, out the back door,
and into the crowded kitchen across
the hall—whose door happens to be

open and where some sort of family
reunion or something is going on
and a female NCO-type is urging
everyone to come in and be seated,
and so you follow into the adjoining
room, are seated, and starting helping
yourself from various bowls handed
round, meanwhile making small talk
with those on each side—a fat man
with a cold and a woman who suspects
her son has not married wisely—
and joining in the general laughter
at the jokes of a horny-looking man
spilling food at the far end—which
proves a mistake because as your
head is back in mirth, a hard roll
smotes you on the shoulder and you
can't decide whether it was thrown
by the small boy behind the peas
or the thirtyish woman with slattern
eyes who keeps looking over at you,
and who either by design or accident
slips into the chair on your right
when dessert is over and everybody
is herded into an ashtrayed parlor
to watch slides of the host's recent
trip to Columbus, Ohio: which slides
go on and on until you begin losing
interest and stick your hand up into
the beam of light and start making
shadow animal heads while everyone
either laughs or whispers, "Ssshh,"

and the host says, "Okay, let's knock
it off," but you don't and he says
it a couple more times, and you
hear even the horny-looking fellow
and the small boy and the woman
with slattern eyes join in with,
"Hey, enough is enough," and so on,
but you keep doing it until the host
moves cursing to a wall and turns
on the overhead light just as you
softly click the front door shut
and hurry across the hallway
to knock upon its twin.

Epilogue

I have just joined a raggedy line
of refugees at dusk. It is raw weather;
the day was a foul wet breath. Tonight
may bring the first snow: if not, tomorrow.
The land is flat—treeless, mud.

These people are carrying things. Children, blankets.
Saucepans, poultry, books. Some are crying,
some are very old. None are fat. Another
just fell. Most are silent in several languages.
They have read no newspaper in months.
They are waiting to cross a bridge.
By dawn there will be fewer;
by noon there will be more.

The Jump Shooter

The way the ball
hung there
against the blue or purple

one night last week
across town
at the playground where

I had gone to spare
my wife
from the mood I'd swallowed

and saw in the dusk
a stranger
shooting baskets a few

years old maybe
thirty-five
and joined him didn't

ask or anything simply
went over
picked off a rebound

and hooked it back up
while he
smiled I nodded and for

ten minutes or so we
took turns
taking shots and the thing

is neither of us said
a word
and this fellow who's

too heavy now and slow
to play
for any team still had

the old touch seldom
ever missed
kept moving farther out

and finally his T-shirt
a gray
and fuzzy blur I stood

under the rim could
almost hear
a high school cheer

begin and fill a gym
while wooden
bleachers rocked he made

three in a row from
twenty feet
moved back two steps

faked out a patch
of darkness
arched another one and

the way the ball
hung there
against the blue or purple

then suddenly filled
the net
made we wave goodbye

breathe deeply and begin
to whistle
as I walked back home.